Parade Float Designer

ODD JOBS

VIRGINIA LOH-HAGAN

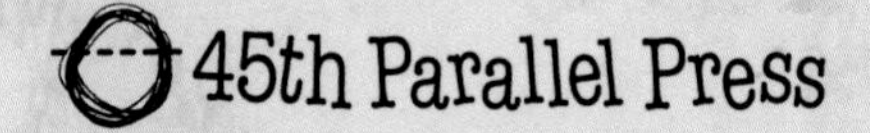

Published in the United States of America by Cherry Lake Publishing
Ann Arbor, Michigan
www.cherrylakepublishing.com

Content Adviser: Brent Amacker, Mardi Gras float designer, Brentoons Media, Mobile, Alabama
Reading Adviser: Marla Conn, ReadAbility, Inc.
Book Design: Felicia Macheske

Photo Credits: © Brian J. Abela/Shutterstock.com, cover, 1; © Cheryl Casey/Shutterstock.com, 5; © Marie Appert/Shutterstock.com, 6, 15, 21, 29; © McCarthy's PhotoWorks/Shutterstock.com, 9; © ZUMA Press, Inc/Alamy, 11; © Robert Crow/Shutterstock.com, 13; © Cafebeanz Company/Dreamstime.com, 16, 17; © John Lambert Pearson/www.flickr.com/CC-BY-2.0, 19; © Paul Bersebach/ZUMAPRESS/Newscom, 22; © Sukpaiboonwat/Shutterstock.com, 25; © Everett Historical/Shutterstock.com, 26; © ARENA Creative/Shutterstock.com, cover and multiple interior pages; © oculo/Shutterstock.com, multiple interior pages; © Denniro/Shutterstock.com, multiple interior pages; © PhotoHouse/Shutterstock.com, multiple interior pages; © Miloje/Shutterstock.com, multiple interior pages

45th Parallel Press is an imprint of Cherry Lake Publishing.

Library of Congress Cataloging-in-Publication Data

Loh-Hagan, Virginia.
Parade float designer : odd jobs / Virginia Loh-Hagan.
pages cm — (Odd jobs)
Includes bibliographical references and index.
ISBN 978-1-63470-027-6 (hardcover) — ISBN 978-1-63470-081-8 (pdf) — ISBN 978-1-63470-054-2 (pbk.) — ISBN (invalid) 978-1-63470-108-2 (ebook)
1. Parade floats. 2. Parade float designers—Vocational guidance—Juvenile literature. I. Title.

GT3980.L65 2016
394'.5—dc23

2015008265

Cherry Lake Publishing would like to acknowledge the work of The Partnership for 21st Century Skills. Please visit *www.p21.org* for more information.

Printed in the United States of America
Corporate Graphics Inc.

Contents

Chapter 1
Making People Happy 4

Chapter 2
Working All Year 8

Chapter 3
Who Doesn't Love a Parade? 14

Chapter 4
Designing Dreams 20

Chapter 5
History of Parade Floats 24

Did You Know? 30
Consider This! 31
Learn More 31
Glossary 32
Index 32
About the Author 32

CHAPTER 1

Making People Happy

What is a parade? What is a float? Why do people create floats?

Imagine a baseball field driving down your street. Anything is possible in a **parade**. Parades celebrate special events. Parade **floats** are decorated stages that move. They're built on anything with wheels.

"At the Ball Game" is a float that's 36 feet (11 meters) long. It's in the Macy's Thanksgiving Day Parade. It's over three stories tall. It's as wide as three buses. It has baseball fields and bleacher seats. Most Americans love baseball.

Macy's hires parade float designers. Amy Kule is the director. She said, "Everyone who participates has this sense of joy, this sense of pride with what they're producing."

Parade float designers make people happy. They create cool floats.

Parade floats have meaning. Designers help people share their messages.

Sikh Americans had a float in the Rose Parade. They wanted people to learn more about them. After the attacks on September 11, 2001, they were treated badly. The float reflected their 125-year history. Minu Kaur Singh said, "We have to share the story of who we are and how long we've been in this country."

Rose Parade floats are seen by 700,000 people at the parade and 55 million people via TV.

Spotlight Biography
RAUL RODRIGUEZ

Raul Rodriguez created more than 500 parade floats for the Rose Parade. His parents recognized his art talent. He said, "My mother wouldn't erase the drawings I did on the dining room wall." He started designing floats at age 15. He entered a high school contest. He designed a Rose Parade float for the city of Whittier. He won. He said, "Early in my life, I got to see my imagination become reality." He received a scholarship for art school. He started his own company. He recreated exotic locations from all over the world. He won many awards for his designs. He had a pet bird named Sebastian. It rode with him on his Rose Parade float. He died on February 18, 2015. He was 71 years old.

Singh drew a timeline of their history. Michelle Lofthouse used Singh's drawing. She created a float called "A Sikh American Journey." The float used 20,000 flowers. It had a temple. This reflected their religion. It had trains, tractors, fruits, and vegetables. Sikhs helped build railroads and farms in America.

Working All Year

What do parade float designers do? What are sponsors? What do parade float designers need to consider? What materials do parade float designers use?

Designers start working when parades announce **themes**. Themes are topics. Designers work year-round. They research ideas. They plan designs.

Floats are designed for events. Sometimes they're made of natural things like flowers. These only last several days. Parade float designers love what they do. It's okay that some creations have short lives.

Macy's parade float designers create floats for Thanksgiving. Their **studio** is in New Jersey. A studio is a place to work. The floats are too big and tall to travel. They have to be taken apart. Each float is built in smaller pieces. Parade float designers think about this.

Macy's Parade Studio has a large room for building floats. It has areas for sculpting, woodworking, engineering, molding, painting, and costuming.

Floats have **sponsors**. Sponsors are people who pay for the work. Parade float designers work with sponsors. They help come up with ideas.

Parade float designers draw their ideas. They make a model. They consider the float **vehicle**. A vehicle is the car, truck, or trailer. This determines how big the float can be.

Parade float designers think about the **frame**. This is the float's skeleton. Frames are covered with foam. They're secured with wire. They're painted.

Parade float designers think about colors. They think about **textures**. Textures are how things feel and look. They consider special effects. Some have included roller coasters, cars changing into spaceships, and water slides.

Parade float designers create something that promotes the parade theme and the sponsors.

Advice From the Field

DON DAVIDSON

Don Davidson designs parade floats. He's done this for more than 40 years. He focuses on his clients. He designed a float for an ice cream company. He created a huge pink hippo. Its mouth released balloons. Davidson named him Bubbles. He wants people to talk about his floats. He said, "To have a float go down the street and have your name mentioned once, and you've spent $200,000 ... is a waste of money. You have to make sure your name is mentioned many times." He designed a float for a fan company. He created a huge ship. It broke a height record for the Rose Parade. Stunt men hung from the ship's poles. They fought with swords on the deck. Parade float designers should make designs that get attention for their clients.

Parade float designers consider materials. They use materials from old floats. They use other materials. They use paper, cloth, and wood. They follow parade rules.

In the Rose Parade, float designers must use natural materials. Many parade float designers use flowers.

They use thousands of flowers. Some designers use dead flowers.

They use dry materials. They use bark, dried grasses, and seeds. The seeds attract birds. Designers have to keep the birds away.

They get creative. They use walnut shells and cornmeal to create skin. They use oatmeal to create animal fur.

Parade float designers use all kinds of materials to create details.

CHAPTER 3

Who Doesn't Love a Parade?

Why do people become parade float designers? What are props? What is the difference between professional and volunteer parade float designers?

Charles Meier fell in love with parades. He was 9 years old. He watched the Rose Parade. He loved the colors. He knew he wanted to be a parade float designer.

He drew float designs. He studied flowers. He memorized parade rules. He put a green blanket over his jungle gym. He stuffed flowers into it. It looked like a parade float!

At age 11, he helped decorate a float. At age 13, he became the youngest parade float designer in the Rose Parade.

Meier's new piece is a huge "firebird". The wings spread to 30 feet (9 m). It includes fire. The bird seems to come to life.

Parade float designers are inspired by parades. Meier said parade floats remind him there's beauty in the world.

Parade float designers make their imaginations come to life.

Blaine Kern has been making art since he was a kid. He painted a big picture in a hospital. This was to pay for his mother's bills. A doctor liked his work. The doctor hired him to create a Mardi Gras float. Mardi Gras is a parade in New Orleans.

One float led to another. Kern became known as "Mr. Mardi Gras." He created big floats. He made big, fancy decorations.

Kern's floats have many **props**. Props are objects. He made big heads. He made a long sea monster. He made giant alligators and gorillas.

Kern's parade float building is a family business. His son and two daughters work for Kern Studios. They happily design floats every day of the year.

WHEN ODD IS TOO ODD!

San Antonio hosts the Fiesta Flambeau Night Parade. They have a special parade float. It's on a 24-foot (7 m) trailer. It carries the parade's queens. It was stolen! It was in a fenced-in area. A lock was cut. John Melleky is in charge of the Fiesta San Antonio Commission. He said, "This is the first time we know of someone stealing a [Fiesta] float." (The previous year, the float was reported missing. It turned out to be a mistake. The school district had the float.) The float is worth about $35,000. It's brightly colored. It has a large guitar, piñatas, and other decorations. It looks like an outdoor court on wheels. Who would steal a parade float?

Jennifer O'Connor helped design a float for the Rose Parade. She learned from her father. She started working on floats at age 13. She said, "I love being part of something so big. There's nothing else like it."

Her float celebrates her hometown. **Volunteers** built it. Volunteers are not paid. They donate their time.

O'Connor said, "Creating Rose Parade floats is a 13-month process. And it starts with choosing the design." Her float is called "To the Rescue." It shows a shark trapped in a fishing net. Smaller sea creatures are saving the shark. Fish scales are made from lime slices. A lobster is red bell peppers. Sand is cracked wheat and cinnamon.

Some parade float designers are volunteers. They build floats to celebrate their hometowns.

Designing Dreams

What are some examples of float designs?
Who is Tillman?

Gilliam is a white whale float. It was built in two parts. It has a 25-foot (7.6 m) body. It has a 25-foot (7.6 m) tail.

Gilliam is a combination of two design ideas. One group designed a thundercloud. Another group designed a whale. Josh Pitts thinks combining the two designs made sense. He said, "All of us, at times, have looked up in the clouds and seen animals."

Pitts and his team used bamboo and pipes. They created a frame. They covered it with wire and cotton. They used laptop screens to make the whale's eyes.

Parade float designers can create whatever they want. They can let their imagination run wild.

The heaviest float in the world is called "Surf's Up!" It featured Tillman. Tillman is a skateboarding dog. The float was 119 feet and 7 inches (36.4 m) long. It weighed more than 100,000 pounds (45,359 kilograms).

The float had a beach. It had a wave pool. The pool made 65-foot-tall (20 m) waves. Tillman and six dogs surfed waves during the parade. The dogs trained for three months.

Tim Estes is president of Fiesta Parade Floats. His company designed the float. The sponsor shared his idea with Estes. Estes loved the idea. But he was challenged by the design. The extra weight and length made the float harder to move.

Tillman is a dog who can surf.

THAT HAPPENED?!?

Hua Tiande broke a world record. His team created the longest parade float. It had 345 sections. It measured 2,596 feet and 9.35 inches (791.5 m). Tiande is from Fujian, China. The parade float was a dragon. It was featured in the Chinese New Year parade. Thousands of strong young men held it up. The dragon's head was 6.6 feet (2 m) high. It had a red ball in its mouth. A band played drums and gongs. Gongs are cymbals. It rained on their parade! By the end of the parade, almost half of the sections were damaged. The damaged parts had to be taken away from the total record-breaking length.

History of Parade Floats

What is the history of parade floats? What is the history of parades? How did parades develop in the United States? Who is Isabella Coleman?

Parade floats developed in the Middle Ages. The Middle Ages lasted from the fifth to the 15th centuries. Churches created religious scenes on wagons. These were stages for traveling religious plays.

The first parade floats floated. People decorated **barges**, or big boats. This was for royal celebrations.

Emperor Maximilian of Germany hired an artist to design "**triumphal** cars." Triumphal means the celebration of victories. The cars were for his parades in 1515. They were pulled by horses. People decorated the cars.

Early parade floats were decorated barges.

The first parades may have started in Nice, Italy. These events inspired parades like Mardi Gras. There are more than 50,000 parades in the United States.

Parade floats became part of American life in the early 1800s. Mobile is a city in Alabama. It hosted its first parade with floats on New Year's Day in 1831. New Orleans hosted its first Mardi Gras parade in 1857. It had two floats. Ak-Sar-Ben is Nebraska spelled backward. It's a parade. It started in 1895. It was the first to use electricity to light and move the floats. The floats used the city tracks. It used power from the wire.

People have been enjoying parades for a long time.

Parade Float Designer

KNOW THE LINGO!

Balloon: something that is inflated or blown up with air

Chassis: the skeleton of a man-made object; the underpart of a vehicle

Den: a large warehouse where floats are built and stored

Dismantler: a person who takes apart the parade float

Falloon: combining a float and balloon, putting a balloon on a rolling or moving platform

Flambeau: flaming torch, associated with night parades

Floral sheeting: petal paper, used to cover the top and sides of a float

Maskers: people wearing masks or costumes in parades

Parade route: the path of the parade

Procession: traveling in a line on a route

Production: business of building floats

Throws: things thrown from a parade float

Pasadena is in California. It hosts the Rose Parade. The first parade was in 1890. It featured many floats. Early floats were simple. Families tied flowers to the wheels and benches of carriages. The flowers were picked from gardens.

Isabella Coleman started designing Rose Parade floats at age 14. She created many **techniques**. Techniques are methods or tips.

She created a **cockpit**. This was a special seat for drivers. It was built into the float. She used airplane wheels. This kept the floats low to the ground. The floats looked like they were floating. She put flowers into glass containers of water. This kept flowers fresh.

Her ideas inspired other designers. The job of parade float designer became important. Parade float designer is an odd job. But it can be very rewarding.

The Rose Parade has many amazing floats.
They all use flowers for decorations.

DID YOU KNOW?

- The Macy's Thanksgiving Day Parade was canceled during World War II. People didn't want to waste materials. Rubber and helium were needed to make war supplies.
- The phrase "Let's have a parade!" is trademarked by Macy's. This means people need permission to use this phrase. They have to always give credit to Macy's.
- Disney Festival of Fantasy is a popular parade. It features Disney characters from more than a dozen stories. They're featured in nine parade floats.
- The Rose Parade and Rose Bowl Game have a "Never on Sunday" rule. The events are held on January 1. If the date falls on a Sunday, it's changed. This is an old rule. The goal was to not scare horses. Horses used to be tied outside local churches.
- The Battle of Flowers Parade is important to San Antonio. The city closes schools and businesses to support this parade. It began more than 120 years ago. It honors those killed during the battles of San Jacinto and the Alamo.
- Zundert is a small town in the Netherlands. It's the birthplace of Vincent Van Gogh. It hosts a flower parade in September. It started in 1936. The parade floats are fantastic. The floats are about 65 feet (20 m) long. They're about 30 feet (9 m) wide. The parade float designers can do whatever they want.
- Parade float designers ensure the floats will last during the parade. The engine is cooled by a large radiator. This prevents over-heating. Tires are filled with foam. This is to prevent flats. Two or more drivers are hidden within the float. This is so they can control the float's direction.

CONSIDER THIS!

TAKE A POSITION! Some people think parade floats waste natural resources, specifically flowers. Florists make money from the parade business. So, florists like parade floats. Some people think parade floats aren't worth the time and effort. What do you think about parade floats? Argue your position with reasons and evidence.

SAY WHAT? There are many parades. Learn more about two parades. Explain the purposes of the parades. Explain how they are similar and how they are different.

THINK ABOUT IT! There are many parade float designs. Learn about some of these designs. Learn about the parade float designer's inspiration. If you were asked to design a parade float, what would you design and why? Remember that you have to follow rules. You have to consider available resources.

SEE A DIFFERENT SIDE! There have been some accidents during parades. Parade floats have crashed into each other. People have fallen off parade floats. Attendees have gotten hurt. Parade organizers provide security. They try to keep people safe. Parades are celebrations. They should be fun. But, they should also be safe. Planning for parades is not all fun and games. If you were planning for safety, what would you think about?

LEARN MORE

PRIMARY SOURCES

Thanksgiving Day Parade Tech, a video about the parade float designers of the Macy's Thanksgiving Day Parade: www.history.com/topics/thanksgiving/history-of-thanksgiving/videos/thanksgiving-day-parade-tech

SECONDARY SOURCES

Heiligman, Deborah. *Celebrate Independence Day.* Washington, DC: National Geographic, 2007.

Sweet, Melissa. *Balloons over Broadway: The True Story of the Puppeteer of Macy's Parade.* Boston: Houghton Mifflin Harcourt Books for Children, 2011.

WEB SITES

City of New Orleans—Mardi Gras Information and Updates: www.nola.gov/city/mardi-gras/

Macy's Thanksgiving Day Parade: http://social.macys.com/parade/

Tournament of Roses: www.tournamentofroses.com

GLOSSARY

barges (BARJ-iz) large boats

cockpit (KAHK-pit) special seat for the driver of a vehicle

floats (FLOHTS) decorated platforms built on anything with wheels

frame (FRAME) the skeleton of the float

parade (puh-RADE) a public celebration where people walk or march in a line

props (PRAHPS) objects

Sikh (SEEK) a person who follows a religion from India and covers their hair

sponsors (SPAHN-surz) people or companies that pay for a float

studio (STOO-dee-oh) place to work

techniques (tek-NEEKS) methods or tips

textures (TEKS-churz) how something feels or looks

themes (THEEMZ) topics or subjects

triumphal (trye-UHMF-ul) victorious

vehicle (VEE-hi-kuhl) a car, truck, or trailer

volunteer (vah-luhn-TEER) someone who donates his or her time, not a professional

INDEX

Disney Festival of Fantasy, 30
dog, 22

float designers
  how to become one, 14–19
  what they do, 8–13
floats, 4–7
  examples of designs, 20–23
  history of, 24–28
  how they're made, 9–13
  world records, 22, 23

imagination, 16, 21

lingo, 27

Macy's Thanksgiving Day parade, 4–5, 9, 30
Mardi Gras parade, 17, 26

parades, 4–7, 15
  history of, 24–28
props, 17, 30

Rose Parade, 6–7, 12, 14, 15, 18–19, 28, 29, 30

sponsors, 10, 11

themes, 8, 11
Tillman, 22

volunteers, 18–19

ABOUT THE AUTHOR

Dr. Virginia Loh-Hagan is an author, university professor, former classroom teacher, and curriculum designer. She loves parades, especially marching bands. She lives in San Diego with her very tall husband and very naughty dogs. To learn more about her, visit www.virginialoh.com.